D1487584

PRESENTED TO:

_____

BY:

_____

DATE:

_____

OCCASION:

_____

ALSO BY JUNE COTNER

Animal Blessings

Baby Blessings

Bedside Prayers

Bless the Day

Comfort Prayers

Family Celebrations

Forever in Love

Graces

The Home Design Handbook

House Blessings

Looking for God in All the Right Places

Mothers and Daughters

Pocket Prayers

Wedding Blessings

Wishing You Well

MIRACLES
OF
Motherhood

PRAYERS AND POEMS FOR A
NEW MOTHER

JUNE COTNER

CENTER
STREET

NEW YORK   BOSTON   NASHVILLE

Center Street®

Hachette Book Group USA

1271 Avenue of Americas, New York, NY 10020

Visit our Web site at www.centerstreet.com.

Center Street® is a division of Hachette Book Group USA. The Center
Street name and logo are trademarks of Hachette Book Group USA.

Printed in the United States of America

First Edition: March 2007

10 9 8 7 6 5 4 3 2 1

ISBN-10: 1-931722-92-7
ISBN-13: 978-1-931722-92-6
LCCN: 2006928722

Illustrations by Rose Lowry

For my dear, sweet granddaughter,
Shay Kelly Casey

Thanks

I am deeply grateful to my children, Kyle and Kirsten, for all the love, inspiration, and welcome challenges they have given to me as a mother. Without them and the precious moments we have shared, this book never would have been possible.

As ever, I'm most thankful for the constant encouragement, patience, and love of my husband, Jim. He remains by my side as I continue to learn and grow as a wife and mother.

I'm greatly indebted to my talented agent, Denise Marcil, who has guided me through so many projects from concept to completion. I owe much of my success to her tireless work on my behalf.

Special thanks go to Rolf Zettersten, publisher of Center Street; my attentive editor, Chris Park; and the tireless, committed people at Hachette Book Group USA: Chip MacGregor, associate publisher; Lori Quinn, associate publisher, marketing; Preston Cannon, director, advertising and promotion; Jana Burson, director of publicity; Penina Sacks, production editor; and Kelly A.

Berry, editorial assistant. With time and attention, they have helped this book grow to its fullest potential.

I feel incredibly lucky to have so many talented writers who contribute to my collections. Only a small fraction of work by new and regular contributors appears on these pages, but even writers who aren't represented have touched me with their words. I agonize over each piece I'm unable to include.

I am also blessed with a special community of book lovers that continues to support my work. I'm particularly indebted to Suzanne Droppert, owner of Liberty Bay Books, who has given me much more than a venue for sharing my work with the community. The staff at the Poulsbo library also deserves recognition for their continual assistance in providing books that have aided and inspired me in my many projects.

Finally, I thank God for blessing me with the miracle of motherhood and guiding me in the work I love.

Contents

New Baby *35*

A Letter to Readers

If you are reading this letter, you are most likely a new mom or just about to become one. Congratulations! Motherhood is a journey that will change you in the deepest and most surprising ways.

Miracles of Motherhood will be the book you turn to when you want to relish your new life with your wonderful baby. Each time I gave birth, I couldn't sleep for two nights because I was so excited. My daughter said that she had the very same experience when her baby girl was born. We both could have used this book during those initial sleepless nights!

This book is filled with prayers and poetry from mothers who have collectively experienced every aspect of motherhood. *Miracles of Motherhood* celebrates the joy and overwhelming love associated with being a mom; it also provides gentle encouragement during the sometimes heart-weary times of motherhood. My hope is that each entry will impart greater insight into your own relationship with your baby.

Once I became a mom I started seeing myself and the world differently, and I viewed other moms with a new level of respect. There is no other role in life where your desire to succeed is so strong that it makes you feel incredibly secure, yet sometimes filled with self-doubt. There is no parenting book that can produce just the right results for your child. Parenting is unpredictable. You summon patience that you didn't even know you had. Being a mom is hard—but also extremely gratifying. Nobody can move you, complete you, strengthen you, or make you laugh like your child. If you succeed as a mother, which you will, the rewards are endless.

My sincere desire is that *Miracles of Motherhood* will provide comfort, insight, and inspiration for the incredible journey of motherhood ahead of you. Indeed, it is a miracle! God bless you and your magnificent baby.

PREGNANCY

EXPECTING

Bless me, Lord, for a new life lives within me.
Allow me to carry this infant
in my body without danger or pain.
Grace us with a healthy child,
rich in spirit and joy.
We thank you, God, for the miraculous creation
we have conceived of our love,
for the sacred life I carry.
May this new being travel on wings of kindness.
May our love always be with this child.

—*Linda Goodman Robiner*

HELLO

little one,
mystery guest
lodging in my womb.
I await your appearance
with great impatience.

Do you hear
my voice as I sing
a lullaby and rock
you in your perfect cocoon?

Will you have my eyes
and your father's ears?
I wonder, as you send ripples
across my universe.
I am humbled by God
for this perfect gift, you.

—*Shirley Kobar*

A Single Heart

May the babe that dwells within me, Lord,
in strength and wisdom grow;
swaddled warm within your loving arms
like a baby long ago.

With your presence too inside me, Lord,
deep in my heart to stay;
stand guard upon each bloss'ming child,
both babe and me, I pray.

Nine months too short a time to share
the baby, you, and me;
please grant our hearts still beat as one
throughout eternity.

—Karen Ganon

GROWING PAINS

Dear child,
pushing, stretching,
anxious to be free
of your confinement,
wait . . . please,
just a little longer.
This moment
will never come again;
let me cherish it,
remember it,
praise God for it,
before you say goodbye.

—*Mary Lenore Quigley*

❦

As a mother comforts her child,
so will I comfort you...

—Isaiah 66:13 (NIV)

❦

Longing

It is said:
the moon reflects in ten thousand streams.
This dream reveals herself
in my rippling veins and bloodpulse.
Girl-child, you and I are
and yet are not separate things;
we indulge in the proximity of skin
and share in one life process.
I know sometimes that
the shallowest river is still too wide to cross,
but we move, one toward the other—
water lapping shore.
I wait at this side of joy, longing to be close.

—*Anita Punla*

Movement

Sometimes we require the softest sounds—
chimes and prayerflags in wind;
one moth humming in dark air.
Tonight, for the first time,
I felt your fluttering wings;
I held my breath; both of us waited.
No other movement came,
but that one rising of air was enough.
You moved and I recognized your touch.

—*Anita Punla*

Our Love

Our love
has merged inside me—
urging an existence,
a minuscule inkling
surging
towards life.

Combining our bodies,
our minds, our hearts
with creativity . . .
Together we're stepping
one generation closer
towards eternity.

—*Anne Selden Annab*

HEART BEAT

I live happily enough in the world;
already my heart runs wild.
But now your presence changes my being:
my center is lowered, stance wide,
a foothold to draw strength from earth.
My womb thrums with your pulse,
beating twice as fast as mine.

—*Anita Punla*

ANTICIPATION

Fluttering, fragile, waiting within your body,
A body that now carries hope within your womb,
A miracle soon to emerge into your world.
And you wonder if you are prepared for the challenge.
The life within brings an inner beauty and grace
That enhances what you are already becoming.
The gift of motherhood is precious.
Be still and listen to your heart, for it will tell you
That the greatest of all blessings is that of motherhood,
And the most wondrous creation of all is that of birth,
Emerging from the cocoon: new life, fluttering free at
    last.
Time and faith, patience and love, anticipation and
    realization.
This new life will be a part of you and your heart
    forever.

—*Judith A. Lindberg*

Pregnant Night

Silently laboring above me,
the moon continues her ancient cycle,
shedding and renewing herself
like the lining of the womb.
I find strange comfort in her perpetual change.
Constancy lies within her variations.
Powerful in this pattern, she has mystified souls for ages.
Her endless courtship with the sun
causes oceans to pull and heave,
devouring stone, eroding sediments,
creating landscapes, birthing continents.
Tonight, she is as full as I.

—*Christy Lenzi*

GIFT FROM HEAVEN

The flowers have their haloes on,
The winds of spring are strumming,
Music is inside of me,
I have a baby coming!

I've never felt this way before,
I always feel like humming,
Dear God, You're giving me a gift,
I have a baby coming!

—*Marion Schoeberlein*

Expectant Mother's Meditation

New-loved and eager soul, it's time. Come slide
into my waiting arms from heaven down
the Milky Way. May all that I provide
for your dear life humbly suffice to crown
your brow of otherworldly preparations
so that your time with us might well fulfill
your destiny's exalted expectations.
To this high end I turn my bending will.

—*Maureen Tolman Flannery*

GREAT BLESSING

It's a mystery
this gift
of joined flesh
made manifest.
Lord, thank you
for your great blessing,
and we ask you
to bestow upon us
the grace
to teach our baby
love and understanding
with every act we do.

—*Shirley Kobar*

BIRTH

CONNECTED

My body takes me through layers of labor,
but I am comforted by the cadence of your voice
as you quietly coach me to breathe.

A swirl of feelings fills me,
and your face tells a story of reassurance
that dispels my fears.

When the urge to push overwhelms me,
I feel your presence as a steady pressure
holding my hand.

Attention floodlights on me,
but we cross into parenthood together—
blest to share a newborn bond.

—*Rebecca K. Wyss*

THE WONDER OF YOU

Never could I have imagined
the miracle inside of me.
Never could I have fathomed
how wonderful you would be.
Never could I have assessed
the richness of your worth.
Forever will I cherish
the wonder of your birth.

—*Jill Noblit MacGregor*

Just Beginning

You rounded
between the covers
of flesh and heart.

I listened,
talked to you,
waited to feel
your fingers in mine,
your mouth at my breast—
a conversation
just beginning.

Came the hour
when you pushed,
urgent to be born,
through the grasp,
pant, and thrust
of my body.

Now I sing the letters
of your newborn name
and cry *Glory*.

—*Joanna M. Weston*

PREPARED CHILDBIRTH

I learned every lesson in Lamaze:
how to focus on a picture instead of the pain;
how to pant and blow instead of scream.
For weeks, I practiced daily:
counting, breathing, timing, pushing—
preparing for the event which still surprised me
when the pressure of the head
crowning through the cervix;
the strangling tightness in my belly,
even blood vessels popping in my face
were nothing compared
to later sensations
of bursting inside
with love for a child
I did not need practice to hold.

—*Jacqueline Jules*

I can do everything through him who gives
me strength.

—*Philippians 4:13 (NIV)*

LABOR'S PAIN

I had no idea
it would be like this,
that I could live
through so much pain,
or feel such relief,
at the sound of your cry.

Love overwhelms me
with one look at your face
and I drown in thoughts of
what I would not do for you,
no suffering too great,
no trial too severe,
no distance too far
that I would not travel
to save you, my own,
my precious child,
my creation of love.

GOD told them, "I've never
quit loving you and never will."
    —JEREMIAH 31:3 (THE MESSAGE)

—*Sally Clark*

FIRST BORN

I heard you cry
before I saw
your wrinkled face,
the nurse's smile
like a benediction
saying it was okay
for me to cry as well.
When she placed you
in my arms,
tears of joy fell
silent as summer rain.

—*Rosalie Calabrese*

NEWBORN

Newly born—
so fresh!
Clean, free,
open to unlimited potential—
what truth!
You are absolute trust,
total love, pure, good,
unconditional perfection.
Powerful beyond proportion,
in your first hours you
bestow immaculate joy,
miraculous peace.
You are at this moment precisely
who you are meant to be.

—Deb Baker

THE BIRTHING

She journeyed down at her own pace;
I paced myself to her rhythm.
She pushed—I pushed.
She crowned—I was crowned.
She was born—I was reborn.
She breathed—I was breathless.
She cried loudly—I cried softly.
I held her—she held me
For the rest of our lives.

—*Donna Wahlert*

AFTERBIRTH

I cannot fathom
The strength of this cord

Binding my life with yours
It envelops every waking moment,
Trespassing even unto deepest sleep

With what love must it be fashioned
That it does not tear apart
From stress and strain
Of this world's travails

Nor does it fray
Even years after it ceases
To serve its purpose

I cannot fathom
The strength of this cord

—*Monica E. Smith*

A Tiny Star

A tiny star rose to Heaven
      and there took the shape of a newborn babe,

  heart beating,
    eyes open,
        and arms reaching out for love.

—*Linda Robertson*

COME FORTH

To Birth: to bring forth, to give rise to.

I birthed you at dawn
when river waters take the first light.
You entered my life,
sun into quiet stream,
with infant down,
a hint of remembering in your eyes.

We birth each other anew daily;
coos and sighs lure into play.
We interweave:
winter and spring, current and wind,
sun and fog,
both of us carrying seeds of joy
ready to sprout:
to scatter,
to come forth.

—*Anita Punla*

Beloved and Blessed

To be blessed to have a little one
To cuddle and embrace
Is the substance and the evidence
Of God's amazing grace.

*Now faith is the substance of things
hoped for, the evidence of things not seen.*
    —HEBREWS 11:1 (KJV)

—Anne Penrod

I think, at a child's birth, if a mother could ask a fairy godmother to endow it with the most useful gift, that gift would be curiosity.

Eleanor Roosevelt (1884–1962)

GETTING TO KNOW A NEW DAUGHTER

Drowsy with birth,
pink and new,
as untried as February's
first push of crocus green,

she stares at me
with one eye barely open,
as if to ask,
how gentle are your hands,
how soft your chest,
how steady your heartbeat?

Over the months
she will learn my voice,
know my touch, the love I hold.
For now she wills herself
to open both eyes
and look me full in the face.

I can wait for her smile,
the clasp of her fingers
around mine—she the teacher,
I a willing student.

—*Connie Jordan Green*

BIRTH DAY PRAYER

May you know the warmth of God's love
reflected in family, friends, and everyone you meet.
May you know the beauty of God's love
in the wonders of our world—
sunsets above mountains,
the silence of snow.
May you know the joy of God's love
in the little things—
a smile that is shared,
a gentle touch.
May you know the peace of God's love
every day of your life—
from dawn that speaks of new beginnings
into the shadowed night.

—Theresa Mary Grass

NEW BABY

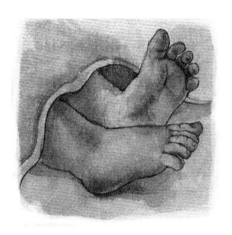

AN INFANT'S PRAYER

I am small,
please hold me.

When I'm peevish,
soothe me with your song.

When I'm frightened,
remind me that you're there.

When I'm flailing,
surround me with your love.

When the world is too big,
please find me.

When you count your blessings,
let me be your heart's desire.

—*Kate Robinson*

SLEEP CYCLE

I awaken from my night visions
of all-consuming passion.
A tiny cry in the night beckons me
and I answer.
Alone with you, I realize,
though helpless, you control me.
Without power, you provide my strength.
Wordless, I understand and learn from you,
everything.
Quiet and contented,
I return to my bed, my slumber,
to drift back into my night visions,
and dream once again
of you.

—*Robin Svedi*

A Promise of Love

As you begin your journey
I can see my reflection in your eyes.
Every time you smile
I know my heart beats because of you.
I will give you the best life has to offer and
you will always know my love.

You will never have to worry about the rain
or be scared of the dark.
I will give you kisses of faith and hugs of grace,
and in my arms you will be safe.

I promise to support your dreams,
nurture your talents, and encourage your spirit.
You are everything that is genuine and true,
and the world is more beautiful because of you.

As you search to make your place in this world
know that anything is possible.
Aim for the stars and trust your instincts.
Expect miracles and all good things will be yours.

—*Lori Eberhardy*

Let Him See for Himself

As I look at this wondrous little being,
I think he has my eyes.
He definitely has his daddy's nose.
He is blessed with his grandma's smile.
He is a part of all of us, as we are all a part of him.
I know now that family is truly interwoven
through all of us,
but help me to remember he is a distinct, unique
    person.
He may have my eyes but prefer to look beyond my
    perspectives.
He may have his daddy's nose but develop none of his
    interests.
He might keep his grandma's smile but find humor in
    different places.
And that will be okay.
He is exactly as he was created.
He is exactly who he is supposed to be.

—*Donna Gunnels*

Instructions for the New Mother

Give up your calendar and clock,
start flowing with milk time.

Hunt for the frayed scraps
and threads of your fears.
Wrap your child's cries around
the skein of your days.

Stop racing to meet your familiar ways—
know change
will always beat you.

Lower that small fist of resistance
still struggling to rise within you—start now—
unclench your life.

—Andrea Potos

My Baby

When I gave birth to you
I had no idea just how much
a baby would change my life,
how often thoughts of you
     would l e a p
        into my heart,
pushing everything else aside.

Somehow, you have managed
to dilate my eyes, so that
everything I see in this world
is filtered by my love for you.

—*Susan R. Norton*

On Baby's Birth

Your miracle at last is here,
the blessing that you hold so dear.
May your joy and wonder linger
as you count each little finger
and touch that tiny, button nose
while on your way to counting toes.

Inspection done, at peace you lift
your glistening eyes toward Heaven's gift
with tears of thanks to God above
for giving you this child to love.
Your happiness is understood,
you've just discovered Motherhood!

—*Barbara Nuzzo*

SHE IS NOT SO SMALL

I am in constant awe that I had a part in her arrival.
As I count every graceful finger and every delicate toe,
and I admire every tiny eyelash,
let me remember that, as she is still so very small in this
    vast world,
her possibilities are equally as vast.
She will become as big as her surroundings allow.
Let me knock down the walls,
let me give her space,
let me help her to grow.

—*Donna Gunnels*

MY GIFT

Although you were
not born
of my body,
it made
no difference,
you see.
I loved
you all
the more
when you
were given to me.

—*Joan Noëldechen*

Baby Blessings

As you gently rest in my arms I can feel
my heart embracing this sweet new life.
As you breathe I hear a joyful noise.
Each new breath becomes a lullaby and
I realize you are breathing to
the rhythm of my heart.

I touch your hand and as your tiny fingers
gracefully wrap around mine,
I pray that you will never let go.
I look into your eyes and as you drift off to sleep
it's a comfort to know that
everything is as it should be.

Each night I listen to the stars
whisper your name and with each new day
I join the angel's applause for the gift of you.
I memorize every detail from your nose
to your toes and I hope that you will
always know love.

Today I promise to hold your hand,
cradle your heart, and lead you down a path
of all that is good and true in this world.
And I pray you will always remember that
you are the best part of me.

—*Lori Eberhardy*

NOT TO WORRY

Your milk will come in,
Your pain, subside.

Your company will leave,
and they'll come back.

Your husband will love you,
and you'll love him.

Your laundry will fold,
your belly, flatten.

Your baby will cry,
your baby will grow.

—*Maryanne Hannan*

In the sheltered simplicity of the first days
after a baby is born, one sees again the
magical closed circle, the miraculous sense
of two people existing only for each other.

−*Anne Morrow Lindbergh (1906–2001)*

NEW BEGINNINGS

No, nothing has prepared you for this—
this strong, sudden surge
of LOVE rushing through you.
Filling empty spaces
you are just now discovering you've had,
rising, then falling with short baby breaths;
as you finger each finger
and kiss all ten toes,
you are cradled in the knowing
that a miracle has been passed
from God's hand to yours
by the reflection you see
in your baby's eyes,
of you, a newborn mother!

—*Anne Calodich Fone*

WONDER

I touch
your skin, soft like velvet,
rub my finger across your cheek, amazed.
Once again, a babe is in my arms.
You flail a bit, then settle,
learning to trust me.

—*Eve Lomoro*

FIRST BATH

Who is more nervous I can't tell.
I immerse you in water,
hold your bobbing head afloat.

My hands tremble under your body,
skin slippery as you wriggle.
You gasp with surprise, then relax.

Blue eyes widen as you drift
into some watery recollection
of our first connection.

—*Mary Kolada Scott*

Thank You

Someone else
could be holding this bundle,
touching a tender cheek,
listening to happy gurgles,
witnessing a toothless smile.

Yet she found the strength
to release to another
what she could not nurture.

May she know in her heart
that the precious gift
has found love in our home.

—*Joanne Keaton*

NEWBORN

Soft as a warm bun,
you rise in your basket:
your yeasty breath,
sweet as morning;
your face, a road map
about to be traveled;
your eyes, clean as the rain:
nothing on this earth is quite so new—

—Barbara Crooker

The Unfamiliarity of Wakefulness

Waking from a deep dream
to unfocused darkness, I turn
toward the window's starry light
and slowly come to comprehension.

The nightstand. The dresser.
My husband tossing beside me.
I am comforted by the gradual fall
of the familiar into place.

This is the way it must be
for my new son who looks out
from his bunting in confusion
and wonder. He has no words

for what he sees, yet
he is adjusting to sunlight
and the mobile of clouds
and rainbows above his crib.

Already he is forgetting
the place he has just come from,
and settling into
the wakefulness of this world.

—*Judi K. Beach*

Just After You Were Born

Just after you were born
I held you close and kissed your sweet face,
my tears of joy mingling with your tears
of surprise and confusion.

I gazed at your eyes, dusky blue,
still holding the mysteries
of your life before birth . . .

felt your first breaths,
warm and sweet against my cheek . . .
beheld your smile, soft and sleepy,
greeting me as if you already knew me.

Just after you were born
I felt your fingers grasping one of mine,
holding tightly to your new world . . .
heard your heart, beating quickly
with the excitement of living . . .
touched your hair, barely there,
angel soft, just a whisper fuzzing of the
gold yet to come.

Just after you were born
I held you close and kissed your sweet face,
and whispered in your tiny, shell-shaped ear,
"Welcome, little one, you are home."

—*Susan Kneib Schank*

For Sleep

Oh, God, though I am a mother,
tonight let me also be your child.
As I have done so many times
for my own precious children,
Lord, bathe me gently,
kiss me sweetly,
sing me a soft, old song
whose words promise
that you will stay beside the bed
of my exhaustion
until safe in your arms
I can drift into a night
of blessed baby sleep.

—*Anne McCrady*

BABY

New
     gift
that you are.
Baby,
you come from
     God,
a blessing.
Birth
like a flower
opens us up.

—Paula Timpson

What Do I Do Now?

This miracle
nestled against me,
warm and comforting
as he is comforted;
sleepy and satisfied
after nursing.

My arms hold a small parcel
which contains so much;
the love of his father and me,
our genes,
and those of our parents
and of their parents and . . .

This new little person
holds so much promise.
Years from now he will leave us
to lead his own life.
But now he depends on me.
He has so much to learn

and so have I.

—*Shirley Nelson*

GRACE

Perhaps I will forget
your warm, wrinkled
body next to mine,
the way you are wrapped
like a wonton in pink and white,
tiny dark curls of hair
sweeping over your brow,
your toes pushing out
in search of the walls
which once cocooned you
close to me, your mouth
opening in a circle
as if the world rests
there for a minute and then
your first hungry cry.
But, Lord, let me
always remember
this moment of grace
when you reached down,
placed this fragile,
undeserved gift
in my arms.

—*Nancy Tupper Ling*

The Newborn

*Teach a child how he should live, and he will
remember it all his life.*
    —Proverbs 22:6 (TEV)

Innocent and helpless infant,
    unaware of the world outside,
    needs loving, feeding, changing, rest.
Nestled in your arms, safe from harm,
    to be nurtured and loved.
    You will guide, shape, teach this little one.
Boundaries placed in both your lives
    will help this baby find his way
    as he will desire to imitate you.

—Pamela Rosales

You and the Stars

The warm bundle,
restless in your arms,
knows little more
than the comforting rhythm
of your beating heart,
a familiar lullaby sung to her
since before her first breath.
She feels the same safety,
the same nurturing love,
wrapped around her now.
Isn't it wonderful
you and the stars
have stayed awake
to keep her company?

—*Mary Lenore Quigley*

Dear Special Child

You are everything there is,
and everything that will be.
You are the sun, the wind, the moon;
you are the earth and the sea.

You are the quiet sounds of night;
the spirit of each day.
You are the sum of the total parts;
you are work and play.

You're the warmth in mommy's heart,
the sparkle in daddy's eye.
You are the lump in everyone's throat
before the tear in an eye.

You are the cool of autumn,
the beauty of the flower.
You are the magic moments
that combine to make an hour.

You are laughter in a room;
you are merriment and mirth;
so to you, dear special child,
I bid you, welcome to Earth.

—*Linda Robertson*

The Gift

A child is born.
A gift to you
wrapped in heavenly blessings.
May your arms
cradle her in life.
May your voice
offer her guidance.
May your gentle touch
help her blossom.
But most of all—
may God's precious love
adorn her with wonder
and purpose.

—*Leslie Neilson*

BABYHOOD

When First I Held You

When first I held you,
the wonder of your arrival
filled me with awe.

You were—and are—
such a miracle to me!
I had such high hopes
and fervent prayers
for you, and I still do.

You teach me something
every day,
and you remind me that
prayers and hopes
are often surpassed.

I am so thankful
to be your parent—
and I'm blessed
to have a child
like you.

—Dena Dyer

The First Year

You make my whole world
brand-new again.
I share your wonderment
at all you see
for the very first time:
raindrops sliding down
a windowpane,
a snowflake brushing
your tiny nose,
a butterfly spreading wings
before your astonished eyes.
I follow your delighted gaze
to a dog's wagging tail
or a just-opened flower.
To you, everything
is miraculous and new.
I see and share your joy,
but most of all I see
the miracle that is you.

—*Sheila Forsyth*

Treasured

May my child rest
as the apple of Your eye

and sleep in the hollow
of Your hand,

guarded by the shadow
of Your wings.

*Keep me as the apple of
your eye; hide me in the
shadow of your wings.*
    —Psalm 17:8 (NIV)

—*Joanna M. Weston*

MINDFUL

Let me hold you, and be mindful,
you are a prayer, born from the most
sacred places of my heart.

Let me listen, and be mindful,
your tears are words,
you are yet to learn.

Let me watch you, and be mindful
that your curious gazes,
will one day follow, with brave footsteps.

Let me love you, and be mindful
that you are always and forever, mine.

—*M. J. Young*

NEW MOTHER IN SEPTEMBER

She remembers when she sank alone
into the grass sprinkled with fallen
leaves curled like the newly born, when she napped
warmed by early autumn.
This year she brings her child
to gaze with her
into a sunburst sky of maple and oak.
She cannot look for long; the child
is lifting fingernails of dirt to her mouth,
the child is dragging a twig
seriously close to her eye.
The mother must dart her eyes,
look and switch, scamper
back and forth between
her daughter and the sky,
stashing images
like a squirrel gathering nuts for the winter—
cache of simple beauty,
necessity of autumn fire.

—*Andrea Potos*

Into the Night

I bathed the child at dusk,
his chubby body pale
in the round tin tub, his pink
buttocks gleaming as the sun
went down.
      Beyond us
the sea hurled foam
on the sand; the pines
darkened like old men
keeping watch as the child
splashed and laughed
into the night.

—Penny Harter

SWEET LOVE DIVINE

Holding this sweet little bundle
of innocence and trust
snugly and warmly to breast
brings me close
as is humanly possible
to understanding
the mysterious beauty
of sweet love Divine.

—*Cindy Chuksudoon*

Are You a Bird, Little One?

You pump both little arms and coo, dove-like,
your bright eyes clear on your destiny—
still a mystery to me, but not you.
You pronounced it yourself,
months before you were born,
with that slight flutter,
the quickening you flew within me as if you had wings.

To your delight,
I gently lift you, hold you tight,
and fly you—
zoom through the kitchen,
zoom through the living room,
zoom through the bedroom.
I land you safely in your crib
and you coo again.

This much I know:
your buoyant spirit makes my heart soar.

—*Susan Koefod*

A Fascinating Thing

It is a fascinating thing—
your hand fisted close.
Fingers yield suddenly,
expose fine branches against rough bark.
You stare for minutes at your open palm,
reading your life,
then gaze into my eyes,
pulling sap from deep within me,
seeking a clearer reflection of who you are.
My child, even the moon
rests only momentarily as leaf-shine,
and reflection is not the moon itself.
You mold your body
into my curves and crevices, but
my breasts are a temporary haven;
milk lets down as leaves to your wind.
And this hand you so surely press against
is only one tree in the forest—
but, yes, rooted thick, rooted deep for leaning.

—*Anita Punla*

EXPECTATIONS

Like prophets of old
we watch for signs,
keys to unlock
our daughter's future.

The way she smears
bananas around
her hands and face
paints an artistic future.

When she snuggles
with me behind
a colorful book,
she is a lover of words.

And we pray the dimple
on her left cheek
guarantees your smile
and a lifetime of joy.

We ponder these things
as she sleeps in her crib.
But what we treasure:
a big smile, a gracious hug,
given freely come morning.

—*Nancy Tupper Ling*

PERFECTION

Ten little fingers and
ten little toes,

soft little cheeks
of perfect pink rose,

fragrant perfume
of warm baby's breath—

I in my rocker,
you at my breast.

—*Mary Maude Daniels*

There's Something About a Baby

There's something about a baby
    that brightens up a room,
for wherever there's a baby,
    smiles just seem to bloom.
They're the center of attention,
    that no one can deny.
They're extremely nice to cuddle
    especially when they're dry!

They're a heavenly creation
    made of God's finest clay.
They're a cause for celebration
    on an ordinary day.
They're the nearest thing to heaven
    found upon this earth,
for they're innocent of sin
    at the moment of their birth.

They're a blessing in a bundle
    wrapped in pink or blue,
and hands that rock the cradle
    receive a blessing too.
There's something about a baby
    too wonderful to describe,
and there's nothing like a baby
    for keeping love alive!

—*Clay Harrison*

When You Need to Rest

Little babies
need you
around the clock.

Perhaps it's then,
through sleeplessness,
that you learn
how strong you are.

—Susan Landon

A Love Poem

Loving you this night,
I hold you longer than you need.
It is more that I am being held:
your arms lift to catch mine;
my limbs extend to include yours,
and we reach out to a world,
redwood branch with new spring growth.
So we dance, rock to and fro;
explore our peripheries.
But your breath upon my skin
is a warm wind rubbing earth,
and our edges blur and thin.
Girl, to what binds us,
say yes.

—*Anita Punla*

New Mother's Prayer

Dear God,

I look in the mirror and I barely recognize the woman looking back.

So much has changed since this baby entered my life.

All my relationships are different.

My priorities have changed.

What used to be so important now seems to be of little consequence.

I am so tired; I can't remember the last time I had a full night's sleep.

I have such an amazing child; I never knew love like this before.

And yet, I can't help but ask,

"Who am *I* now that I am a mom?

What has happened to the woman I used to be?"

Please help me as I sort out my new role and my new life.

Please help me to create a new version of me.

Please help me to be both the mother and the woman you want me to be.

Amen.

—Patrice Fagnant-MacArthur

WHEN YOU'RE BLUE

When you're sad,
when you feel all alone,
when you miss
the company of friends,
the laughter that it brings,
and when you long to share
what's in your heart,
then take some time
for yourself.

Let a friend
mind the baby
while you take a walk,
do your hair,
or take a bubble bath.

Your little one
depends on you,
needs your very best.

—*Susan Landon*

Nourishment

I wake in the night to find you
nestled close to me under the quilt,
your tiny hands stroking my arm.

Here, in our dim sanctuary,
you nurse and nurse—
not even opening your beautiful

sleepy eyes, the lids threaded with delicate
blue veins. It's raining outside, holy
water falling from the eaves. At last

you turn, sighing, perfectly content,
your warm milky breaths slow and even.
Those tiny fingers knead my skin

even in sleep. A smile darts across your face,
a dreamy version of your dimpled grin. You're full
of secrets not yet spoken. My fingers lace

through your hair, stroking your fluid skin,
searching out the answers with my fingertips.
Why fine bones broaden in your presence, my son,

and why I find, each time I embrace you,
that I am this porous earth.

—*Leah Browning*

MOTHER'S MIDNIGHT PRAYER

Dear God,
It's the middle of the night and I am up feeding the
    baby.
It is so quiet and peaceful, just my baby and me,
and You, of course, You who see all and know all.
Thank You for this child feeding happily in my arms.
Thank You for these moments of alone time.
Thank You for being here with us in the stillness.

Amen.

—*Patrice Fagnant-MacArthur*

THIS FIRST YEAR

Your eyes meet mine with instant trust.
Friends bring baby gifts to open;
you, dear child, are my truest gift.

People come to see the baby;
you snuggle contented in my arms.
Our precious bond keeps on growing.

Now you reach to grasp my finger
or, lying on your belly, lift
your head, looking around for me.

Treasured months speed by; you're rolling
over, front to back, back to front
and laughing as I cheer you on.

Your longer waking hours give us
time to play, to take strolls and rides,
to rock and look at picture books.

Soon you scoot yourself by inches;
later you're crawling room to room,
trailing me, exploring with glee.

You pull yourself upright one day.
Jabbering in joy, you take your
first step, toddling into my arms.

—Marjorie Gray

TODDLERHOOD

Prayer for the Toddler's Mom

Remind me, God, that he is not finished yet.
When he tests me and I grow intolerant,
bless me with patience.
Let my example be a good one.
Help me discipline this child with affection.
Should I grow angry, let me guard against unkindness.
Support me in helping him to be curious,
to sample the wonders of the world.
When I find motherhood frightening,
grace me with strength.
Bless me with energy to do this urgent work.
When I forget that he is only a child, help me
to remember.

—*Linda Goodman Robiner*

Today He Is a Toddler

Today, he has tantrums,
scatters toys, spills food,
refuses to sleep,
demands your undivided attention,
makes you crazy.

On some tomorrow, he will calm your outbursts,
help tidy up, prepare the food,
lose sleep worrying about you,
give back the undivided attention that you bestowed
    upon him,
be your sanity in an insane world.

Today, he gives kisses, cuddles, and hugs,
brings laughter to your heart,
creates a memory each moment,
brings everything into focus.

On some tomorrow, he will have the same abundance
    of love,
will still make you laugh,
will be your living memory book,
a constant reminder of important things.

In the meantime,
just enjoy today.

—*Sandra McGarrity*

My Daughter

Soon enough my daughter will know
that this world is not entirely made of
    butterflies and caterpillars,
    long walks near pebbled streams,
    picnics and teeter-totters,
    blowing bubbles,
    or sweet songs and kisses.
But during these years—these precious years—
let me drink in and enjoy
    her giggles and laughter,
    ruffles and bows,
    drawings for Mother,
    birthdays with playmates,
    sweetness and innocence.
And may these memories linger,
helping us both through
    the difficult years
    that surely will come,
    bridging childhood to adulthood,
    where we will bond again—
    this time, as friends.

—*Janice Jones*

PRECIOUS GIFTS

Funny faces,
toothless grins,
kissy feet,
chubby limbs.

Holding hands,
endless tickles,
bearish hugs,
smiling dimples.

Bath-time bubbles,
birthday wishes,
bedtime stories,
good-night kisses.

—*Shaunda Kennedy Wenger*

Little One

Sleep,
cradled in God's love.

Crawl.
Feel earth's pulse nourish
your every breath.

Stand.
Meet the world eye to eye.

Smile,
gather your courage,

then
run with the wind.

—*Mary Lenore Quigley*

Baby Steps

Today we both take baby steps.
Holding my breath, I watch as
you walk away from me.

While you learn to walk,
I am learning to withstand
all my fears about what's ahead for you
along life's way.

You trip over a toy car and
cry out for me.
You allow me a brief hug
before breaking away to try again.

You turn awkwardly to search
my face for approval,
only to tumble again.
This time you giggle and
this time I smile.

—*Susan Koefod*

Reflection

As I reached for your hand today
to help you down the stairs,
your smile was so fast and true
it could only have come
from the moment of your creation.
You looked so deeply into my eyes,
you turned me around until
I saw just what you were seeing:
your mommy, richly colored
with every shade of pure
two-year-old love.

—*Deb Baker*

Under Your Wing

God,

   Gather me under your wing, for I am in need of some mothering myself. Assure me when I take first steps into motherhood and fall. Comfort me when I skin my heart. Soothe me when I am pushed beyond my limits. Guide me in this tug-of-war between my self and my new role as Mother.

   Give me peace. Create peace through me.

Amen.

—*Britt Kaufmann*

TODDLER

She takes naps to recharge,
you take naps to shut down.
She wears purple tights,
you wear control-top hose.
She sings in the grocery store,
you wait for the privacy of the shower.
She takes an hour to eat,
you scarf down food in between clients.
She loves the box,
you like the present.
She talks to everyone,
you wait to be addressed.
She questions everything,
you question nothing,
except why you can't be more like her.

—*Deborah Finkelstein*

CHRISTENINGS

PROMISES

To You, Holy Father,

We promise to give our best care and guidance to the beautiful child You have given us to raise. We thank You for him and say that we want him to love and serve You all his life.

We lean on Your grace and guidance, Your provision and promises.

We can promise to give him what he needs for this life, but we need to ask You to give him meaning, and eternity.

We love You.

Your servants, in this and everything.

To you, little one,

We promise to pray for you; listen to you; discipline you; kiss and cuddle you; give you good food; play games with you; make sure you're educated; buy you clothes; watch over your safety; teach you to count, cook, and drive; release you into adulthood; support you always . . .

We hope many things for you, little one, but beg for only one: that you know the joy of the life that comes from Christ.

We love you.

Your parents, now and always.

—*Elizabeth Adam*

A Christening Blessing

Blessed be _____
who brings joy into the world,
whose birth gifts us with new graces,
whose very breath takes us
to new places.

Praise be the goodness
from whence such blessings flow.
Praised be all
who nurture this child,
who help her grow.

—*Mia Schmidt*

BABY BLESSING

As an acorn grows into a maple tree,
may the gifts inside you blossom.
May the Lord watch over you
all night and all day
and bless you with ease of well-being.
May you be free from danger.
May God bless your physical being
with good health
and your spirit with abundant happiness.
May your life be a path with heart.

—*Linda Goodman Robiner*

The Baptism

The infant boy, seven weeks old,
startles into screams as he's immersed
birth-naked in the ornate silver font,
thrice-repeated before dripping baby
finds comfort in his mother's arms.

Darling boy, you cannot yet know we
only do what we know to keep you safe,
expanding the circle of your protection,
entrusting your life to Heaven's care
as well as our earthly own.

—*SuzAnne C. Cole*

A Dedication Prayer

Heavenly Father of Our Family,

We promise to take care of this precious child for You. We promise to pray for her. We promise to teach her Your ways and Your Word. We promise to love her as You love us.

We ask You to give us wisdom, strength, and compassion. We ask You to protect her in every way throughout her life. We ask You to lead her into a life of loving and serving You. May she be Yours forever and be everything You intend her to be.

—Elizabeth Adam

CHRISTENING BLESSING

Dearest Father in Heaven,
Bless this child and bless this day
of new beginnings.
Smile upon this child,
and surround this child, Lord,
with the soft mantle of your love.
Teach this child to follow your footsteps
and to live life in the ways of
Love, Faith, Hope, and Charity.

—*Author unknown*

REFLECTIONS

A Blessing for Our Children

Blessed be our children
who take us out of ourselves,
who teach us,
even as they grow from us.

—*Mia Schmidt*

MOTHER TO MOTHER

When I sit and rock my baby,
I often think of you.
And I imagine,
you must have felt this way, too.

By your fine example,
I've become the woman I am today.
I felt your love for me
even when you did not say.

Through your actions, you showed me
to be kind, giving, and fair.
And now with my own daughter,
these attributes I will share.

Thank you, my dear mother,
for all you've done and all you do.
I hope my daughter will know
such a loving, selfless mother as you.

—*Deborah Warren Craig*

Heartfelt Question

If I extend the fingers of my love,
to touch a child and name him for my heart,
and wind his brow with countless rainbow ribbons
of bedtime stories,
and wrap his heart in soft chiffon
by fountainings of givings—
what will he offer back?
Does love grow love?

—*Sylvia Wave Carberry*

A Baby Inspires Us . . .

to give without being asked,
to protect without hesitation,
to love without limit.

—*Janet Lombard*

In Passing

Have you not, on your separate sojourns,
passed each other, you and my mother,
she getting used to the heavens,
you to the confines of matter;
she, soul spent, seeing her life in retrospect,
burning for all that remained,
you keeping your unborn vigil
at the gate of pain?
Did you know each other by your ties to me,
she who'd once housed my body within hers,
you who sought time
and permission to enter through mine?
Were there messages, tasks she passed to you,
she leaving, you coming to earth,
things she'd forgotten to teach me
to ease the tight toil of your birth?
What is your mission among us,
fine first daughter in a house of men,
next link in the great unbroken chain
of mothers since our mother earth began?

—*Maureen Tolman Flannery*

MIRACLE

We begin life as a miracle
and slowly forget
that we still are.

—*Corrine De Winter*

GENERATIONS

Gazing at your tiny head,
it's not always you I see.

Instead, I can imagine
my mom holding me,
just as her mother
must have cuddled her.

One day you may embrace
a babe of your own—and
now and then think of me.

—*Joanne Keaton*

INSPIRATION

For Life

The world
is a wondrous place
to raise children.
Some days
I would run
with the deer and fawn
for joy.
Bless us with courage
to abide in the world,
and teach our children
to acknowledge
the grace of life.

—*Shirley Kobar*

MANY HEARTS

You will never learn so much
as God intended
than from a child.
Listen to them.
Love them with all of your being.
Teach them peace and compassion,
and know that when you do these things
you are reaching out not to one,
but many, many hearts.

—*Corrine De Winter*

LIFETIME BLESSINGS

I'd give you gentle moonlight
and a million stars for dreaming.
I'd give you a flower-strewn path
and petals that sprinkle ease for your journey.
I'd give you birdsong and carefree days.
I'd give you a world of rainbows, if I could,
and a magic wand to grant your every wish.
But I'll do what I can, every day that I can,
with all my love.

—*Judith A. Lindberg*

THE PICTURE OF HIS LIFE

Each and every newborn
is given a most precious gift
a magnificently **blank** canvas
on which to paint the picture
of his life. We can either help
or hinder in this new creation.

So beware of every word
and action directed to a child.

You are providing
a canvas of possibilities,
adding paint for his palette,
handing him a sable brush
of encouragement, giving
your love and inspiration
for his life's masterpiece.

—*Susan R. Norton*

You

Ever may I be blessed with the strength
to be true and wise, accepting of our weaknesses,
to walk with you in turmoil and to share your grief,
to cry with you,
to laugh with you.
Ever may I be moved by the sweetness of the sharing
of this gift,
this moment,
and all the moments that transcend time:
You.

—*Nancy Early Byron*

Children are the anchors that hold a
mother to life.

—*Sophocles (c. 496–406 B.C.)*

Family Tree

They say it goes back generations,
first growing in another nation
far from where we call home now.
Great-great-grandparents,
crossing mountains and miles of blue,
found this new land, a place to be free,
came carrying seeds here. . . .

Then a dream come true:
you,
my new leaf
on our family tree.

—Arlene Gay Levine

CELEBRATION

I want to celebrate you.
I am truly blessed to be a part of your world.
I learn from you, I admire you, I love you.
You are my own personal star that follows me
around and shines down on me.
You light my life with magic and wonder.
Such a gift of love.
You are a part of my soul.
You own a piece of my heart.
Your loving spirit provides a constant parade
of emotions that warm my heart.
I feel complete knowing you are near,
feel empty without you.
I want to celebrate you,
yesterday, today, and tomorrow.

—*Lori Eberhardy*

Blessed Light

Blessed child, blessed light,
In my arms this blessed night.
Hold you warmly, hold you tight,
Blessed child, blessed light.

Full of sunshine, full of joy,
Blessed child, blessed boy.
Full of wonder, full of light,
Blessed child, blessed night.

—*Charles Ghigna*

NEVER-ENDING STREAM

When you give away things,
whether money or other objects,
they are gone forever.
But not love—the more you give,
the more your heart fills with it.
Love is a never-ending stream.

—*Amma*
(translated by Janine Canan)

The very fact that God has placed
a certain soul in our way
is a sign that God wants us to do
something for him or her.
It is not chance;
it has been planned by God.
We are bound by conscience to
help him or her.

Blessed Mother Teresa (1910–1997)

For My Daughter on Her Twenty-first Birthday

When they laid you in the crook
of my arms like a bouquet and I looked
into your eyes, dark bits of evening sky,
I thought, *Of course this is you,*
like a person who has never seen the sea
can recognize it instantly.

They pulled you from me like a cork
and all the love flowed out. I adored you
with the squandering passion of spring
that shoots green from every pore.

You dug me out like a well. You lit
the deadwood of my heart. You pinned me
to the earth with the points of stars.

I was sure that kind of love would be
enough. I thought I was your mother.
How could I have known that over and over
you would crack the sky like lightning,
illuminating all my fears, my weaknesses, my sins.

Massive the burden this flesh
must learn to bear, like mules of love.

—*Ellen Bass*

A Mother's Prayers

Thank you, Lord,
for the gift of this child.
Bless me today with
the grace of your wisdom.

Bestow your protection
upon this child and me.
Guide us safely along
the path you have paved.

Grant me kindness,
understanding, and patience.
Fill me with love to be
the mother this child needs.

Take my heart and hands,
O Lord, join them with yours.
Help me nurture this child
in your likeness and ways.

—*Katherine Murphy*

MOTHERHOOD

The love of awakened motherhood
is a loving compassion not only for one's own children
but for all people, animals, plants, rocks, and rivers.
It is a love extended to all of nature's beings.
For one who has awakened to true motherhood,
every creature is his or her child.
Such love, such motherhood, is divine love,
which is God.

—Amma
(translated by Janine Canan)

HERE IS THE MOTHER AWAKENING

Here is the mother awakening
even as she dreams.
Here is the leap she is taking
where the sky becomes her beams.
She joins the stillness of creation
when she pauses at mid-flight.
She wins the praise and adoration
of all she had to fight.
Here is the mother waiting,
here is her future in the dark.
Here is the discovery she is making,
the dirt she tills at daybreak
where something sleeping wants to start.

—*Cassie Premo Steele*

A Weeping Willow Prayer

Lord, grow our children
like your willow tree
with graceful branches,
each chain bowed,
weighted with humility.
Sustain their roots in rich
firm soil, their light-green
leaves with full sunshine.
Make their shelter strong,
inviting, for hearts to hang
upon their limbs.

—*Nancy Tupper Ling*

TODAY

Today let us give thanks
for the intricate threads
that weave us together as new mothers.

Let us always cherish
the wondrous, little creations
we hold in our arms.

Let us welcome
into our hallowed hearts
the blessings of this journey.

But most of all—
let us uphold within us
the wondrous miracle of motherhood.

—Leslie Neilson

Author Index

Permissions and Acknowledgments

Grateful acknowledgment is made to the authors and publishers for the use of the following material. Every effort has been made to contact original sources. If notified, the publishers will be pleased to rectify an omission in future editions.

Elizabeth Adam for "Promises" and "A Dedication Prayer."
Anne Selden Annab for "Our Love."
Deb Baker for "Newborn" and "Reflection."
Ellen Bass for "For My Daughter on Her Twenty-first Birthday" from *Mules of Love.* Copyright © 2002 by Ellen Bass. Reprinted with permission of BOA Editions, Ltd.
Judi K. Beach for "The Unfamiliarity of Wakefulness."
Leah Browning for "Nourishment."
Nancy Early Byron for "You."
Rosalie Calabrese for "First Born."
Janine Canan for "Motherhood" and "Never-Ending Stream" from *Messages from Amma,* Janine Canan, ed. Copyright © 2004 by Janine Canan. Published by Celestial Arts. Used by permission of the author and Steven Fleisher.
Sylvia Wave Carberry for "Heartfelt Question."
Cindy Chuksudoon for "Sweet Love Divine."
Sally Clark for "Labor's Pain."
SuzAnne C. Cole for "The Baptism."

Deborah Warren Craig for "Mother to Mother."

Barbara Crooker for "Newborn."

Mary Maude Daniels for "Perfection."

Corrine De Winter for "Miracle" and "Many Hearts."

Dena Dyer for "When First I Held You."

Lori Eberhardy for "Celebration," "Baby Blessings," and "A
  Promise of Love."

Patrice Fagnant-MacArthur for "Mother's Midnight Prayer"
  and "New Mother's Prayer."

Deborah Finkelstein for "Toddler."

Maureen Tolman Flannery for "Expectant Mother's
  Meditation" and "In Passing."

Anne Calodich Fone for "New Beginnings."

Sheila Forsyth for "The First Year."

Karen Ganon for "A Single Heart."

Charles Ghigna for "Blessed Light."

Michael S. Glaser for "A Blessing for Our Children" and "A
  Christening Blessing."

Theresa Mary Grass for "Birth Day Prayer."

Marjorie Gray for "This First Year."

Connie Jordan Green for "Getting to Know a New Daughter."

Donna Gunnels for "She Is Not So Small" and "Let Him See
  for Himself."

Maryanne Hannan for "Not to Worry."

Clay Harrison for "There's Something About a Baby."

Penny Harter for "Into the Night."

International Bible Society for scripture taken from the
  Holy Bible, NEW INTERNATIONAL VERSION®
  (NIV). Copyright © 1973, 1978, 1984 International Bible
  Society. All rights reserved throughout the world. Used by
  permission of International Bible Society.

Janice Jones for "My Daughter."

Jacqueline Jules for "Prepared Childbirth."

Britt Kaufmann for "Under Your Wing."

Joanne Keaton for "Generations" and "Thank You."

Shirley Kobar for "Hello," "Great Blessing," and "For Life."

Susan Koefod for "Are You a Bird, Little One?" and "Baby Steps."

Susan Landon for "When You Need to Rest" and "When You're Blue."

Christy Lenzi for "Pregnant Night."

Arlene Gay Levine for "Family Tree."

Judith A. Lindberg for "Anticipation" and "Lifetime Blessings."

Nancy Tupper Ling for "Expectations," "Grace," and "A Weeping Willow Prayer."

Janet Lombard for "A Baby Inspires Us."

Eve Lomoro for "Wonder."

Jill Noblit MacGregor for "The Wonder of You."

Anne McCrady for "For Sleep."

Sandra McGarrity for "Today He Is a Toddler."

Katherine Murphy for "A Mother's Prayers."

NavPress Publishing Group for scripture taken from *The Message.* Copyright © 1993, 1994, 1995, 1996, 2000, 2001, 2002. Used by permission of NavPress Publishing Group.

Leslie Neilson for "The Gift" and "Today."

Shirley Nelson for "What Do I Do Now?"

Joan Noëldechen for "My Gift."

Susan R. Norton for "My Baby" and "The Picture of His Life."

Barbara Nuzzo for "On Baby's Birth."

Anne Penrod for "Beloved and Blessed."

Andrea Potos for "New Mother in September" and "Instructions for the New Mother."

Anita Punla for "Movement," "A Love Poem," "Longing," "Heart Beat," "Come Forth," and "A Fascinating Thing."

Mary Lenore Quigley for "You and the Stars," "Growing Pains," and "Little One."

Linda Robertson for "Dear Special Child" and "A Tiny Star."

Linda Goodman Robiner for "Prayer for the Toddler's Mom,"
    "Baby Blessing," and "Expecting."
Kate Robinson for "An Infant's Prayer."
Pamela Rosales for "The Newborn."
Susan Kneib Schank for "Just After You Were Born."
Marion Schoeberlein for "Gift from Heaven."
Mary Kolada Scott for "First Bath."
Monica E. Smith for "Afterbirth."
Cassie Premo Steele for "Here Is the Mother Awakening."
Robin Svedi for "Sleep Cycle."
Paula Timpson for "Baby."
Donna Wahlert for "The Birthing."
Shaunda Kennedy Wenger for "Precious Gifts."
Joanna M. Weston for "Treasured" and "Just Beginning."
Rebecca K. Wyss for "Connected."
M. J. Young for "Mindful."

About the Author

June Cotner is a bestselling author, anthologist, consultant, and speaker. Her books include *Graces, Bedside Prayers, Animal Blessings,* and *Amazing Graces* (HarperCollins); *Mothers and Daughters, Baby Blessings,* and *Wedding Blessings* (imprints of Random House); *Forever in Love, Family Celebrations,* and *Comfort Prayers* (Andrews McMeel); *Looking for God in All the Right Places* and *Wishing You Well* (Loyola Press); *Bless the Day* (Kodansha); *House Blessings* (Cotner Ink); *The Home Design Handbook* (Henry Holt and Company); and most recently, *Pocket Prayers* (Chronicle Books).

Altogether, June's books have sold more than 700,000 copies and earned praise in many national publications, including *USA Today, Better Homes and Gardens, Woman's Day,* and *Family Circle*. She has two forthcoming anthologies: *To Have and to Hold* (Center Street) and *Star Light, Star Bright* (Chronicle Books).

June has led workshops for writers and given presentations at bookstores nationwide and at the Pacific Northwest Writer's Association Conference; the Pacific Northwest Booksellers Association Conference; and The Learning Annex schools in New York, San Francisco, Los Angeles, and San Diego. For information on scheduling June as a speaker or workshop leader, you may contact her at one of the addresses listed below.

June is a graduate of the University of California at Berkeley and the mother of two grown children. She lives in Poulsbo, Washington (a small town outside Seattle), with her husband, two dogs, and one cat. Her hobbies include clogging, yoga, hiking, cross-country skiing, and volunteering at her local elementary school.

June Cotner
P.O. Box 2765
Poulsbo, WA 98370
june@junecotner.com
www.junecotner.com